Snakes and ladders

FOR poor producers in the South (another name for the Third World), life must sometimes seem like a game of snakes and ladders — with far more snakes than ladders. It's hard enough producing your commodity in the first place. Your crop may suffer from drought or flood or storm, or be affected by pests or diseases. It may do badly because, through shortage of land, you have to grow it on poor soils. Work in mining and fishing is just as risky — and dangerous too.

But your troubles have only just begun when, despite all the hazards, you have got your product ready for market. Then you find that decisions made in the North (the rich, industrialised world), where your product will eventually be consumed, have fixed a price for your commodity which condemns you to poverty. If you try to diversify into a different commodity, or if you try to add value to your product by processing it yourself, then you come up against new obstacles set up by the rich and powerful.

All you want is a decent return for your effort — enough so that you can look after your family and live in security and dignity. Is it too much to ask? Why is it so hard? And could things be different?

Oxfam and Christian Aid work with the poor of the South. Like the World Development Movement, we also inform the public and decision-makers in the United Kingdom about the causes of poverty, and about changes which could be made in the North to help the poor. In this booklet we explain how the world trading system creates poverty, and we suggest some ways to change it. We also show what you as a consumer can do to make a difference.

Tanzania: cotton is the only source of livelihood for villagers in Shinyanga Region; but they are competing with subsidised cotton farmers in the USA.

Geoff Sayer/Oxfam

A buyer's market

MANY people in the South make their living by producing 'primary commodities' which end up in shops and factories in the North. They grow crops like sugar, coffee, and cotton; or they mine metals such as copper and tin; or they catch fish and shellfish. The South also exports manufactured products such as clothing.

Many farmers, miners, fishing communities, and factory workers in the South are poor because of the low prices paid for the commodities they produce. A low price means hard choices for them and their families — whether they can send their children to school, whether to plant again on exhausted soils, how to survive a drought or a family illness.

Take sugar-cane farmers. Cane sugar is a major export in many developing countries, where it was grown on colonial plantations. After independence, these countries were encouraged to continue growing sugar by the big importers, like the UK. In the mid-1980s the price collapsed and the producers — already poorly-paid — were plunged into unemployment and hunger. Oxfam and Christian Aid help sugar workers to grow food crops on disused land.

Why are prices for sugar, and for most other Southern commodities, so low? It's a matter of supply and demand. When supply is greater than demand, there's a buyer's market and prices are low. When supply comes from the South and demand is in the North, prices are also influenced by inequalities in economic power.

Frances Rubin/Oxfam

Brazil: working on a sugar–cane plantation. Piece–work rates are as low as 30 pence a day.

On the demand side, the amount of sugar eaten in the North is on the decline, partly on health grounds. On the supply side, sugar-cane growers are in a double bind. They are in competition with countless other Southern sugar producers. If over-production drives the price down, they may have no choice but to increase production in the hope of selling more — and that drives it down even further.

They also have to compete with beet sugar, grown in the North, where production is often subsidised. In 1967 the twelve countries which now make up the European Union imported nearly four million tonnes of sugar between them. By the mid-1980s they were net *exporters* of nearly four and a half million tonnes of beet sugar.

Now scientists can make a substitute for sugar out of maize. Much of the maize grown by farmers in the USA is turned into a sweetener to replace imported cane sugar. This is bad news if, like the Philippines, you have traditionally exported your sugar to the USA.

Things are no better if you produce tin — because tin cans are being replaced by aluminium, plastic, and glass; or copper — because copper cables are being replaced by optical fibres. Even if you grow something which isn't being replaced, and can't be grown in Europe or North America, you still have to compete with all the other Southern producers. Tea, coffee, and cocoa are the most obvious examples. Coffee is grown in more than 40 Southern countries.

On top of all the other pressures to export, there is the effect of debt. In 1991 one-third of the export earnings of countries in sub-Saharan Africa and Latin America went towards paying the interest on their international debts. Debt-ridden countries, urged by the banks and international lending organisations (which are backed by powerful Northern governments), are obliged to export more and undercut their neighbours. So prices fall further.

For countries and communities in the South that rely on exporting just one or two commodities, it's a disaster. Their economies are vulnerable to swings in prices beyond their control. And there's another catch: if they try to diversify away from commodities into manufactures, they run into trade barriers erected by Northern nations to protect their own industries.

Bolivia: destitute mining communities are reduced to crushing stones after the collapse of the tin industry.

Jenny Matthews/Oxfam

Power and poverty

ORDINARY people try to make a living growing sugar or coffee in the South. Ordinary people buy sugar or coffee in the supermarkets of the North. Linking them are some extremely powerful companies and important international bodies.

Big companies dominate the trade in many Southern commodities. In some cases — like bananas from Central America — they own and run everything from the plantations themselves, through the shipping lines, to the brand name. In other cases — like coffee — the crop is often grown by small farmers, who sell to local traders; but the market in countries like the UK is dominated by a handful of big companies. Just two companies, Nestlé (with brands like Nescafé) and Philip Morris (with brands like Maxwell House), dominate over three-quarters of the UK instant-coffee market.

The prices of many commodities are set by a different kind of market: by dealings between commodity brokers in London and New York, far away from the control of the countries where they were produced. Fluctuations in these markets are caused not just by supply and demand, but by stock-market ups and downs, elections in the North, rumours, and speculation.

Such things can make the difference between survival and disaster for tens of thousands of poor producers. In one week in 1989 the international price of coffee dropped by one-third. For small farmers in countries like Uganda, which depends on coffee for much of its export earnings, it was devastating.

Haiti: Mrs Berberus Joseph delivers her coffee crop for weighing at a co-operative warehouse in Carice.

The South needs the volume of trade and investment that only big Northern businesses can provide. But the greater bargaining power of those businesses can damage the interests of Southern producers, unless their power is regulated. In fact, not everything is left to the mercy of the market. There have been attempts to stabilise the price of commodities; but because of the pressures to over-produce, these arrangements tend to collapse — as they did for tin in 1985 and for coffee in 1989 —

Carolyn Watson/Oxfam

leading to disastrous falls in prices (which, of course, benefit big business in the North). There are also international organisations which regulate trade, the most important of which is the GATT.

The General Agreement on Tariffs and Trade (GATT) was set up by the major trading countries in 1947 to reduce tariffs and other barriers to trade. World trade has grown as a result, but the fastest growth has been in the trade among the rich countries in manufactured products. The rich have got richer, while most of the poor have stayed poor. Negotiations are dominated by the powerful countries in the North, which insist that poorer countries remove restrictions to free trade; and yet the rich retain such restrictions when it suits them — for instance, by keeping barriers against textile imports from the South.

The latest GATT round — the Uruguay Round — was concluded in December 1993, after seven years of negotiations between more than 100 countries. The GATT has been replaced by a new World Trade Organisation (WTO), which is now responsible for implementing the decisions of the Uruguay Round, including regulations in the 'new areas' of agriculture, services, investment, and intellectual property (patents), as well as trade in goods. It will have more power than the GATT to settle disputes between countries over trade .

While the rich will get richer from the agreement, the very poorest countries will actually lose. The OECD has estimated that the poorest countries stand to lose around £4.7 billion annually, with those in sub-Saharan Africa worst hit. These desperately poor countries must be compensated.

UNCTAD — the United Nations Conference on Trade and Development — was set up in 1964 in response to discontent among Southern countries about international economic relations. It became the forum for global commodity discussions, but has not achieved much, partly because of resistance from rich and powerful countries. It is now little more than an advice-giving body for developing countries. It has no say in forming international policy.

Banana skins

Christian Aid

Brixton market, south London: Mr Edmé Celestine (left) and Mr Anton Bowman, on a fact-finding mission for the Windward Islands Farmers' Association, examine bananas on a stall.

COULD anything be simpler than a banana? It is a tropical fruit, so it doesn't compete with the produce of farmers in the European Union; it is a popular and nutritious food, and unlikely to be made obsolete by a technological breakthrough; people in the South grow and export bananas, people in the North buy them. Surely there are no problems here — no banana skins to slip on?

Unfortunately, there are. Most EU countries import bananas from countries in the South, usually those with whom a trading relationship exists from colonial times. For instance the UK traditionally buys bananas from the Windward Islands in the Caribbean. The small farmers there depend on the crop, just as their country's economy does. For example, Dominica, one of the Windward Islands, relies on bananas for 70 per cent of its foreign-exchange earnings. At present these bananas have preferential access to the UK market, despite being more expensive than bananas from large plantations in Central America — the so-called 'dollar bananas', produced by big US fruit companies.

The prospect of the Single European Market at the beginning of 1993 caused fears in the Windward Islands that their bananas would have to compete with dollar bananas. Customers in Europe might get cheaper

Lomé and the Single European Market
Members of the EU, especially the UK and France, had special trading arrangements with former colonies, and these have been extended by the EU under the terms of the Lomé Convention. This gives duty-free access to the EU for most — but not all — exports from the 'ACP' group of countries (69 nations in Africa, the Caribbean, and the Pacific). However, these arrangements are under threat. Because Lomé favours some countries over others, it comes into fundamental conflict with the GATT, which is founded on an agreement not to discriminate between trading partners. The Uruguay Round, concluded in December 1993, gives all countries improved access to each other's markets. This means that the ACP countries will no longer enjoy preference in EU markets — which, for some goods, will be opened up to non-ACP countries. So the poorest countries have done badly out of the Uruguay Round.

fruit; US companies would probably make more profit; but small farmers in the Caribbean would almost certainly be ruined.

With the help of the Norwich-based development education group, Farmers' Link, Oxfam, WDM, and Christian Aid campaigned in 1992 to persuade the EU to adopt a regime that would continue to protect the ACP banana producers, such as those from the Windward Islands. A new EU agreement on bananas came into force on 1 July 1993. It maintained duty-free access for ACP bananas to the EU, and established mechanisms to regulate the quantity of bananas allowed in from other suppliers. But this agreement was challenged by the governments of the Central American banana-producing countries.

In January 1994 the GATT ruled that the EU arrangements on bananas were illegal under international trade law. It is now only a matter of time before the present arrangement is dismantled; the Windward Islands banana farmers will have to compete for markets with the much larger Latin American plantations. Although the social and ecological costs of production are much higher in Latin America, the financial costs are about half.

Christian Aid and Oxfam support the Windward Islands Farmers' Association (WINFA), which promotes the social and economic welfare of small-scale farmers whose main crop is bananas. Representatives from WINFA have visited Europe to find out the facts about the banana market, which will help them to plan for the future. With the help of Oxfam and Christian Aid, Farmers' Link have set up a Banana Action Network, linking banana farmers in the Caribbean with banana-plantation unions in Central America, to help foster a sense of solidarity rather than competition.

Double standards

Bangladesh: a garment factory in Dhaka.

ALMOST all primary commodities must be processed before being sold to the final consumer. This processing adds value to the raw material, so it sells at a higher price. The more value that is added locally, the better for local producers. But rich importing countries protect their own industries by imposing sliding scales of import duties — tariffs — which increase as more value is added to the product: for instance, the tariff on cocoa beans is 2.6 per cent, but the duty on chocolate is 11.8 per cent. Such tariffs discourage Southern countries from investment in manufacturing, and keep them in the trap of depending on the export of primary commodities.

Non-tariff barriers are used to the same effect. For instance, if a Southern country tries to break away from dependence on primary commodities by moving into manufacturing textiles, it runs up against the Multi-Fibre Arrangement. Under the MFA, Northern countries impose quotas on the quantity of textiles and clothes they import from 27 Southern producers. The MFA, first introduced in 1974, was supposed to be a temporary arrangement to give Northern countries time to restructure

Bangladesh and the UK: some vital statistics (1993 World Bank estimates)

	Bangladesh	UK
Wealth (gross national product per person)	£147	£11,033
Infant mortality rate (children dying in their first year, per thousand)	103	7
Life expectancy	52 yrs	76 yrs

their textile and garment industries to cope with competition from the South. It has been extended five times, until finally in 1992 GATT agreed on a plan to phase it out over ten years, starting in 1995 at the earliest. But that is ten years too late for countries like Bangladesh.

One of the world's poorest countries, Bangladesh relied until recently on exports of primary commodities like jute and tea. In the 1980s it started to move into clothing manufacture, where its cheap labour force gave it an advantage over other producers. The industry has created about half a million new jobs in Bangladesh — mostly for women and children. Conditions are not good: wages are low, overtime compulsory, and health and safety conditions poor. Workers are organising themselves to campaign for better wages and conditions, but it is an uphill struggle while exporters have to compete for space in restricted Northern markets. That's why clothing workers need supporters in European countries to press the EU to lift its quotas on their products. (The Lomé Convention is no help to Bangladesh, because it is not one of the privileged ACP group of countries.)

Bangladeshi garment workers are victims of Northern double standards. The rich and powerful nations of the North argue that trade liberalisation — the removal of trade barriers — is essential. They threaten economic sanctions against countries in the South which erect trade barriers to protect their markets against subsidised exports of Northern agricultural surpluses. And yet they keep their own barriers against exports from the South.

The Common Agricultural Policy (CAP)

The European Union's Common Agricultural Policy aims to protect European farmers. A combination of subsidies and other incentives encourages over-production, which results in the infamous 'grain and beef mountains'. Such surpluses can harm producers in the South when they are 'dumped' on the world market at subsidised prices. The international price is forced down, and Southern producers of these same crops lose income. When grain is dumped on local markets, prices can fall so low that small farmers are ruined; then Southern countries become dependent on cheap but unreliable food imports.

Reforms to the CAP were announced in May 1992, but they failed to end export dumping. Similarly, the GATT negotiations, which included agricultural products for the first time, have failed to tackle the problem.

The Multi-Fibre Arrangement harms the poor and should be ended. Bangladeshi textiles and clothing should be allowed free access to the EU without delay. Northern countries' subsidies for their agricultural exports also harm the poor and should be ended.

Fair trade in action

THE present pattern of world trade is clearly not fair. We — consumers in the rich North — get the pick of the world's crops at cheap prices. Trading companies, most based in the North, make large profits for their shareholders. Meanwhile the producers — families, communities, and whole countries — remain in poverty because of the low prices they are paid for their commodities.

Bolivia: trying out a new spinning machine at the workshop of the Artesanias Sorata Handicrafts Group.

Theresa Stearn/Oxfam

Oxfam, Christian Aid, and the World Development Movement believe that fairer trade means a fairer world. At the end of this booklet we will describe some of the changes in national and international policy that would help to tackle trade-created poverty. But there is also a growing movement to make trade fairer right now, in the everyday purchases that we all make. We all have the power as consumers to choose to buy goods that are traded fairly — goods which give a decent return to the producers in the South. To make that power effective we need information, and we need fairly traded goods to be easily available.

Oxfam Trading, founded in 1965, sells products from the South through Oxfam shops and its own mail-order catalogue. This programme, known as Bridge, is about 'fair trade in action', for Oxfam Trading is an Alternative Trading Organisation (ATO). Another big British ATO is Traidcraft, founded in 1979 and now selling through mail-order catalogues, 2,000 voluntary representatives, and about 70 retail outlets.

Alternative trading began as a practical response by European and US development organisations to poverty in the South. The aim was to create a trade link between producers and consumers which strengthened the position of the producers. Instead of seeking out products from middle-men that can be sold as cheaply as possible in the North, alternative traders seek out groups of producers (usually organised into co-operatives) who need support, and help them to develop products which are paid for at fair prices that directly benefit the actual producers. The traders use the profits to help to improve the skills of the producers, for instance in design and marketing.

ATOs tend to trade mostly in hand-crafted items and textiles, as these are the kinds of product being made by people in the poorest communities in the South. Crafts production fits into the lives of women with children, and agricultural labourers who are employed for only part of the year.

ATOs can make a real difference to people's lives. In Bangladesh, women making jute baskets are able to save for the first time in their lives, and their children, previously in work, are going back to school. Bolivian peasant women are earning twice as much for their hand-knitted sweaters from Oxfam Trading as they were from their previous customers, and are learning how to deal with commercial buyers in the UK and the USA. Tribal people in Thailand and the Philippines have been encouraged to develop new products that will appeal to the growing numbers of tourists who visit the region and are interested in their traditional crafts.

The turnover of Oxfam Trading's Bridge scheme was £9.4 million in 1992/93, and Traidcraft's was £5.8 million. Total ATO turnover in the UK adds up to perhaps £20 million each year. It may seem like a lot of money, but the potential market is enormous, and many more producers could achieve independence if Northern consumers appreciated their skills and were prepared to pay a fair price for them.

Bangladesh: making a sika for sale through the Jute Works, a co-operative that sells to Alternative Trading Organisations in Britain.

Nick Fogden/Oxfam

A new way of doing business

ALTERNATIVE Trading Organisations offer fairly traded goods but, compared with supermarkets and department stores, they offer a very small range of products, and reach only a fraction of the potential market: British shoppers spent £41.7 billion on food in 1990. However, there is a new movement that aims to capture a significant part of that market with fairly traded goods.

Some new initiatives show how fairly traded goods can move from the margins into the mainstream of manufacture and retailing.

Cafédirect is a blended filter coffee sold by a consortium consisting of Oxfam Trading, Traidcraft, TWIN Trading, and Equal Exchange (which are all Alternative Trading Organisations). The coffee is bought directly from three producer co-operatives in Mexico, Costa Rica, and Peru. Since the scheme started in November 1991, they have always received at least 50 per cent above the world market price. The coffee is sold through the outlets of all the consortium members, and also through mainstream shops. The first big supermarket chains to start selling Cafédirect are the Co-op and Safeway. ATOs have sold fairly traded coffee for many years, but the message on the packet always emphasised support for the country of origin — Tanzania or Nicaragua. Cafédirect's more 'up-market' packaging (which won a design award) and its taste — mild Arabica coffee grown on high slopes — enable it to compete on its own merits in mainstream shops, while it carries an uncompromising message about fair trade.

An even more ambitious initiative is the **Fairtrade Mark**, which was launched in March 1994. Any manufacturer marketing a product that originates in the South can apply to an independent foundation (set up by a consortium including Christian Aid, the World Development Movement, and Oxfam) for the right to use the Mark. It is a guarantee that the producers have been paid a fairer price, and work in better than average conditions, with respect for the local environment.

The Mark will not be awarded merely on the assurance of the importer or retailer. The Fairtrade Foundation applies clear and objective criteria, and reserves the right to follow an 'audit trail' right back to the producers in the South, to investigate whether they continue to do well out of the deal.

Cafédirect was the first product to be sold with the Fairtrade Mark, in April 1994, along with Green and Black's **'Maya Gold' chocolate**. On sale in selected UK supermarkets, the chocolate is made from cocoa beans which are the traditional crop of the Mayan people of Belize. Things were getting desperate for them when world cocoa prices plummeted recently: they never knew until harvest time how much they would be paid for their produce. The contract with Green and Black has ended this insecurity. Now they get a guaranteed higher return and a long-term trading agreement.

The Fairtrade Mark means real and direct benefits to commodity producers in poor

Bolivia: Nicholas Porco grows coconuts and cocoa beans on his farm 150km north of La Paz. His cocoa beans are processed by the El Ceibo Co-operative, which sells cocoa to Alternative Trading Organisations in Britain.

Belinda Coote/Oxfam

countries. They are also important as examples of fairer trade: a way of doing business with the South which ATOs and development agencies in the UK, Europe, and North America have been pursuing for years, and is now being actively promoted to mainstream companies. The South needs the trade and investment that only Northern businesses can provide — but on fairer terms.

Recommendations

CHRISTIAN AID, Oxfam, and the World Development Movement have learnt from overseas experience that there is a range of issues which must be seriously considered in order to create fairer trade and help poor producers and the people we work with in the South.

1 The World Trade Organisation
Arrangements should be made to compensate those poorest countries which will be at a disadvantage following the conclusion of the Uruguay Round agreement. The World Trade Organisation should be made more democratic. It should address the wider social, cultural, and environmental impact of trade policies, and should take special account of the needs of developing countries.

2 Dumping of Northern agricultural surpluses
Northern countries, in particular those belonging to the European Union, must end the practice of subsidising their agricultural exports, which results in the dumping of surpluses on world markets in unfair competition with the products of the South.

3 The Multi-Fibre Arrangement
The Multi-Fibre Arrangement should be ended, with support for those countries that will experience difficulties in transition. The EU and UK should monitor the impact of the phase-out of the MFA on the poorest countries. The EU should immediately drop Bangladesh from the list of 27 countries affected by the MFA — in effect, opening the European market to exports of clothes from Bangladesh.

4 Support for Southern commodity producers
The EU should support initiatives to help Southern commodity producers to get higher and more stable prices. They should also use aid and trade support to help these producers to reduce their dependence on selling raw materials.

5 Fair trade in action
Importers, manufacturers, and retailers should respond to increasing public concern about the prices paid to producers in the South, and about the conditions under which production is carried out, such as working hours, health and safety, and the environmental impact of production. They should aim to meet the standards set by the Fairtrade Foundation, and should seek the Fairtrade Mark for their consumer products.

6 Debt
All these reforms should be complemented by further debt relief for Southern countries, so that more of their export earnings can be available for useful investment rather than for debt servicing, and so that the pressure to increase exports, which often causes gluts and forces prices down, is reduced.

What can concerned individuals do? To find out more, please contact any of the organisations listed opposite.

Campaigns for fair trade

Christian Aid

Christian Aid works in over 70 countries, supporting aid projects run by and for local people. It is an official agency of 40 British and Irish churches, and helps poor communities of all religions and none.

Christian Aid aims to strengthen the poor towards self-sufficiency and challenge the structures that keep people poor. For its campaign on international trade, it has produced a wide range of resources which show how trade works against the poor, and explain what can be done to change things — from encouraging consumers to be Third-World friendly to lobbying the European Community to change its agricultural policies.

For more information, contact Christian Aid, PO Box 100, London SE1 7RT. Phone 071 620 4444. Fax 071 620 0719. (Charitable number 258003.)

Oxfam

Founded in 1942, Oxfam is a development and relief agency. It promotes long-term sustainable development, but also provides emergency relief in times of crisis. By funding local groups, regardless of race, sex, religion, or politics, Oxfam supports people's struggle to survive and improve the quality of their lives. Oxfam receives some government funding, but depends largely on voluntary work and donations from the public.

Oxfam puts fair trade into practice through Oxfam Trading, and campaigns internationally for the reform of trade agreements which prevent Southern farmers and manufacturers from competing fairly in world markets.

For more information, contact Oxfam, 274 Banbury Road, Oxford, OX2 7DZ. Phone 0865 311311. Fax 0865 312560. (Charitable number 202918.)

The World Development Movement

The World Development Movement (WDM) is Britain's leading pressure group working for policy changes that directly benefit the world's poor. WDM is totally independent and operates through an expanding nationwide network of members, local action groups, lobby teams, and support staff. It is a democratic movement with a vote for every member.

WDM's trade campaign is pressing the European Union for a speedy end to the barriers against poor countries' textiles and clothing.

For more information, contact WDM, 25 Beehive Place, London SW9 7QR. Phone 071 737 6215. Fax 071 274 8232.

Other resources

Oxfam

■ *The Oxfam Report: It's Time for a Fairer World*, 1991.

■ *The Trade Trap: Poverty and the Global Commodity Markets* by Belinda Coote, 1992.

■ *Oxfam and Trade*, a free leaflet giving facts, figures, and case studies about the world trade system.

World Development Movement

■ *Stop the Stitch Up* Campaign Pack. All you need to campaign for a fairer trade in textiles and clothing.

■ "Stop the Stitch Up" t-shirt (one size fits all).

■ *Threadbare* Report on the effects of the Multi-Fibre Arrangement on the Bangladeshi clothing industry.

Christian Aid

■ *A Raw Deal: trade and the world's poor*, by Peter Madden, 1992.

■ "Trade for Change" — a free campaign pack.

■ "Bittersweet", a video about sugar, available in VHS/PAL, for sale or free to hire.

Roshini Kempadoo/Oxfam

St Vincent: harvesting bananas for export to Europe.